THEN & NOW

COLUMBUS

OPPOSITE: This picture, taken in the 1920s, shows the original headquarters of the Cummins Engine Company, which was located in this house (left) at the east end of Fifth Street. The company's first manufacturing plant can be seen here also, and eventually the old house was completely surrounded by other Cummins buildings. Today Cummins, Inc., still uses this property, but the original building eventually fell into disrepair and was demolished in 2005. (Courtesy of John Rondot.)

THEN & NOW

COLUMBUS

Tamara Stone Iorio

To Chris, whose love and support are never ending.
To Julia, Colvin, Lukas, and Leo, who bring me joy and inspiration every single day.

Copyright © 2010 by Tamara Stone Iorio
ISBN 978-0-7385-7808-8

Library of Congress Control Number: 2009943818

Published by Arcadia Publishing
Charleston, South Carolina

Printed in the United States of America

Then and Now is a registered trademark and is used under license from Salamander Books Unlimited

For all general information contact Arcadia Publishing at: 2009943818
Telephone 843-853-2070
Fax 843-853-0044
E-mail sales@arcadiapublishing.com
For customer service and orders:
Toll-Free 1-888-313-2665

Visit us on the Internet at www.arcadiapublishing.com

ON THE FRONT COVER: These views look south on Washington Street from Fifth Street around 1925 and in the summer of 2009. At right in the early view is the Union Trust building with the St. Denis Hotel and the distinctive clock on the corner. At left are H. L. Rost jewelers and F. J. Meyer Dry Goods. The modern view shows the Union Trust building now occupied by Hilliard Lyons. The building on the left has been replaced and served as the Irwin Union Bank Operations Center until the bank's failure and takeover by First Financial Bank in September 2009. (Courtesy of the Bartholomew County Historical Society and the author.)

ON THE BACK COVER: This view, looking north on Washington Street from Third Street, shows a parade in 1917. The distinctive five-globe streetlights were found all over downtown Columbus in the early 1900s. (Courtesy of the Bartholomew County Historical Society.)

CONTENTS

ACKNOWLEDGMENTS

This book would not have been possible without the help of many generous and knowledgeable people. Thanks first to the Bartholomew County Historical Society, which allowed me access to all the museum's photographs and resources. Julie Hughes and Carla Clark were so helpful with the scanning of the museum's valuable photographs. Thanks also to David Sechrest from the Historic Columbus Indiana Web site, a marvelous repository for all things related to Columbus. The Web site's message board members and the Columbus Indiana Celebration Committee—including George Kelly, John Rondot, Richard Bray, and Jim Loesch—loaned me pictures and offered their expertise for the book. Rhonda Bolner of the Columbus Indiana Architectural Archives was invaluable in my research. Her knowledge of her family history, the Lincoln-Orinoco Company, and Columbus architecture is extensive. She also donated several pictures—both then and now photographs—to my project. Cindy and Freeda at Cindy's Frame Shop were also a great help in unframing and reframing old photographs to make them accessible for the book. (They do great work!) Everyone else who loaned me their valuable old photographs and shared their memories also deserves thanks—Larry Ruble, Shirley Lyster, Dennis and Joyce Orwin, Nick and Cathy Rush, Mark and Marabeth Levett, Melinda Engelking, Jim Holland, Herb and Connie Stiltz, Paul Hodler, Carol Ahlbrand, Hutch Schumaker, Jean Merckel, Pat Zeigler, Terry and Susan Whittaker of Viewpoint Books, the Columbus Parks and Recreation Department, and Tre Bicchieri restaurant.

Finally, thanks to my family, who put up with another few months of obsessive researching and writing, and allowed me to complete another labor of love. I could not have done it without you!

All then images are courtesy of the Bartholomew County Historical Society or the author except for the following: page 3, John Rondot; page 14, Viewpoint Books; page 30, New York City Public Library; page 36, Jim Loesch; page 39, Lyle Cummins; page 47, Jean Merckel; page 49, Tre Bicchieri and Nancy Stevens; page 55, Hutch Schumaker; pages 72 and 73, Columbus Indiana Architectural Archives; pages 82 and 89, Rhonda Bolner; page 83, Cindy's Frame Shop; page 86, Nick and Cathy Rush; page 90, Mark and Marabeth Levett; page 91, Dennis and Joyce Orwin; pages 28 and 75, Carol Ahlbrand; and page 94, with permission from the *Republic* (formerly the *Evening Republican*), photograph by Fred Ellington.

All now images courtesy of the author except for the following: pages 29, 65, 73, 83, and 85, Rhonda Bolner; and pages 27 and 34, Chris Iorio.

INTRODUCTION

The best cities are always growing to adapt to the needs of changing populations. The challenge for these communities is to remember and preserve the best of their history while allowing for this transformation. Columbus, Indiana, is a vivid example of a community that has changed dramatically over the last two centuries while preserving some of its most important historical assets.

What began as a small agricultural town in the 19th century became a thriving manufacturing region in the early 20th century. Early industry in Columbus included mills, furniture manufacturers, an early automobile producer, and the largest tannery in the world. The founding of two different companies in 1919—Cummins Engine Company (now Cummins, Inc.) and the Indianapolis Air Pump Company (later Arvin Industries)—was the start of a new era for Columbus, as both companies became Fortune 500 Companies and were crucial to the growth of Columbus. Not only did these companies provide jobs for many residents of the town, but the companies' leaders were also often community leaders and played important roles in philanthropic ventures in Columbus. One of the founders of Cummins was W. G. Irwin, whose father, Joseph, started a bank in 1871 that was a large presence in Columbus for more than 130 years. Much of Columbus mourned the loss of a community institution when Irwin Union Bank failed in 2009. Although many early names in Columbus business are now gone, Cummins, Inc., is still a vital part of the city. From its humble beginnings, today Columbus is a modern city with a mix of occupations, including agriculture, industry, technology, and health care.

The story of Columbus, however, has some unusual chapters. The city's history includes some visionary leaders whose efforts ensured that this small Midwest city would become an unlikely showplace of modern architecture. The construction of First Christian Church (designed by Eliel Saarinen) in 1942 was the start of an influx of world-renowned architects into Columbus. Today this building is one of Columbus's most recognizable landmarks. Many people who have lived in Columbus all their lives would be amazed to see photographs of the lot where the church now stands in its humble early life as a train depot and then a city park. In the following years, a group of farsighted city leaders (including Joseph Irwin's great-grandson J. Irwin Miller) created a program to continue to attract well-known architects to Columbus. The program was based on the idea that the quality of life in a community was enhanced by the "built environment" in that community. At the start, the Cummins Foundation agreed to pay the architect fees for the designs of much-needed new school buildings, provided the architect was selected from a list of approved, renowned architects. While Cummins has developed a well-deserved reputation for its generosity in supporting community programs, this early program also aided Cummins by making the town a more attractive place for young executives to locate. The program was successful and eventually was expanded to include other public-use buildings as well. In the following decades, the number of buildings in Columbus designed by world-famous architects grew, and in 1991, the city was honored by the American Institute of Architects as the sixth best city in the United States in architectural innovation—behind only Chicago, New York, Washington, San Francisco, and Boston.

While modern architecture has made Columbus somewhat famous, historic architecture continues to hold a prominent place in the city as well. Columbus began its life as a city with a few square blocks of downtown buildings. While many small towns in America have seen their downtowns fall into disrepair, Columbus's downtown has remained a thriving part of the city's identity, with many offices and retail shops occupying buildings that have stood for more than 100 years. Today much of downtown Columbus is listed on the National Register of Historic Places, and several of the city's most recognizable buildings come from the early years of Columbus's history. When Cummins, Inc., built its world headquarters in downtown Columbus in the 1980s, the company chose the site of a 150-year-old manufacturing building. Instead of tearing down the old building, the old brick structure was incorporated into the design of the new building.

Of course, even historic downtown has not been static. Although many old buildings remain, functions and ownership have changed, and new buildings now stand next to many old buildings. Like all cities, Columbus has some areas today that are unrecognizable to those who only knew the city many years ago, and at the same time, other areas are easily recognizable. This book includes old pictures of Columbus compared and contrasted with new pictures of the same locations, highlighting how much has changed and how much has stayed the same. Seeing more clearly the changes Columbus has undergone during the past century may remind us that, with foresight and effort, Columbus can continue to grow and thrive.

CHAPTER 1

PUBLIC BUILDINGS

The Frances Comfort Thomas Home for orphans was built in 1893 on the northeast corner of Illinois and Cherry Streets in East Columbus. The home was surrounded by a large garden and farm, and much of the food for the home was grown in the garden or came from the animals on the property. As many as 74 children once lived here. The building was torn down in 1967.

The Bartholomew County Courthouse was dedicated in 1874 at a ceremony marked by music, speeches, and dancing in the streets that was described in detail in the Louisville newspaper at the time. The building was designed by Isaac Hodgson at a cost of $250,000, thought to be quite an extravagant sum of money. The large clock was installed in the tower in 1875. Although the building was gradually updated over the years, the exterior appearance has remained almost the same, with the exception of the removal of the dormers from the roof.

The county jail was built about the same time as the courthouse and in a similar style. It was located just south of the courthouse. The building included living quarters for the sheriff and his family. It was demolished in 1966, and another law enforcement building stood here until the early 1990s. Today the Bartholomew County Memorial for Veterans—25 limestone pillars erected in 1997—stands in this location.

In the 1870s, the Columbus Post Office was located on Fourth Street, and in the 1890s, the post office was in the 400 block of Washington Street. By 1897, this building (above) at Sixth and Washington Streets was the third known Columbus Post Office and was leased by the government from Frances T. Crump. Multiple horse-drawn wagons carried the mail all over town. Today the building houses Viewpoint Books on the lower level—one of Indiana's oldest independent booksellers—and condominiums on the second level.

The Columbus Post Office and Federal Building was the city's fourth post office and was constructed in the 1920s at Washington and Seventh Streets. In the early 1970s, the post office moved to a larger building on Jackson Street, and this building served for many years as the school corporation administration building. Currently it is owned by a software company and has been converted into apartments for young executives.

The city waterworks and powerhouse was built on the banks of the White River in 1903. A filtering system, developed in 1913, used sand to filter up to 4 million gallons of river water daily, and the building supplied the city's water until the 1950s, when it was replaced by a system of wells. Steam generators in the plant also produced the electricity needed to power early streetlights in Columbus. The building was solidly constructed with a 2-foot thick foundation and 17-inch inside walls. Since the 1970s, it has housed the senior center.

Designed by local architect Charles Sparrow, the old city hall was built in 1895 on Fifth Street. The building was also used for dances, exhibitions, and basketball games over the years, and the city's first library was located there before the Carnegie Public Library was built. A new city hall was erected in the 1980s on Second Street, and the old building was converted into a bed-and-breakfast for many years, although it is currently empty. The old city hall is listed on the National Register of Historic Places.

The original Fire Station No.1 was built in 1895 on Fifth Street next to city hall. It had four paid staff, a fire chief, and 29 volunteers. Originally the building had a tall tower that served as a lookout for smoke and fire, and as a place for wet fire hoses to hang to dry. Horse-drawn wagons were used before the first fire truck was acquired in 1918. The building was razed after a new fire station was built at Eleventh and Washington Streets in 1941.

The Orinoco Fire Station (also called Fire Station No. 2) was built at the corner of Thirteenth and Hutchins Streets and opened in 1909. Originally the building housed three firemen, two horses, and one fire wagon. In 1920, a motorized fire truck was added. The station was retired in 1963 when a new Fire Station No. 2 was built on Central Avenue. Arvin Industries, whose headquarters was located nearby, then bought the building and used it for many years as the acoustical research department.

This building (shown below) was one of the earliest hospitals in Columbus. It was located on Fifth Street from around 1909 to 1917, when Bartholomew County Hospital was built. Originally it was also one of several Reeves family homes that stood on the block in the early 1900s.

The H. C. Whitmer Company bought the property in 1921 and manufactured medicinal products here until the 1950s. The building was torn down in the 1960s for the construction of the Lincoln School, now known as Columbus Signature Academy.

Bartholomew County Hospital was built outside city limits on Seventeenth Street in 1917. In order to make the hospital accessible, Seventeenth Street was extended, and a bridge was built over Haw Creek. Although the hospital location has not changed, the main entrance today is located off of Haw Creek Boulevard, and the name was changed to Columbus Regional Hospital in 1992. A historic flood hit the Columbus area in June 2008 and caused nearby Haw Creek to fill much of the hospital, which was then closed for more than four months.

The Carnegie Public Library was dedicated in 1903 at Fifth and Mechanic (now Lafayette) Streets after philanthropist Andrew Carnegie—who supported libraries all over the country—donated $15,000 to the city. The Tabernacle Christian Church was located just behind the library, which was designed to look like an open book. In the 1960s, the old library was replaced with a new library designed by architect I. M. Pei, and a section of Lafayette Street was permanently closed off to allow for more space. Today the Bartholomew County Library stands here, with sculptor Henry Moore's *Large Arch* in the plaza.

PUBLIC BUILDINGS

CHAPTER 2

STREET SCENES

This view shows Washington Street looking south from between Fourth and Fifth Streets around 1938vv. The Haberdashery Clothing Store and Miller-Jones Shoes are visible on the corners of the next block, and a man (perhaps George Cummins) is standing on the sidewalk on the right in front of Cummins Bookstore, which was located for years at 406 Washington Street. The lower levels of the courthouse are just visible in the distance.

The early bird's-eye view (below) shows Columbus from the top of the courthouse in the early 1890s—after St. Bartholomew's Church was built in 1891 but before city hall's construction in 1895. The early view shows Railroad Square on the right, where First Christian Church stands today. Many buildings are recognizable in both scenes, including St. Bartholomew's, First Presbyterian, the Irwin Home, the White Star Building on Fourth Street, and the Storey Home (now the Visitors Center).

These views look south from Seventh Street on Washington Street in 1920 (above) and today (below). The early view shows the electric cable car lines, streetcar tracks, and the five-globe gaslights common in downtown at the time. The block of buildings on the left is similar in both views, while the houses on the right in the early view are now gone.

These pictures show Washington Street looking north from Fifth Street during an Elks Parade in 1896 (above) and today (below). The early view shows the *Evening Republican* newspaper building on the right. This was one of six newspapers published in Columbus at the time. A restaurant/ saloon is visible on the left, but nothing has been developed on Washington Street north of Sixth Street yet. Today Home Federal Bank is just visible on the right and the former Irwin Union Bank (now First Financial Bank) is visible on the left.

These images, taken during an Elks Parade in the 1890s (below) and the Ethnic Expo Parade in 2009 (above), look south from the northeast corner of Fifth and Washington Streets. A man is visible on a balcony of the first building on the left showing the vantage of the previous page's picture. The building on the left in the early view is a German pharmacy (Deutsche Apotheke), and the St. Denis Hotel (now Hilliard Lyons) and the courthouse are visible on the right.

These pictures show the northwest corner of Washington and Fifth Streets in 1900 (below) and 2010 (above). The earlier image shows a horse-drawn "posting vehicle" used for advertisements and driven by Walter Doup. In the 1890s, the post office was located on this corner, and the letters "PO" can still be seen on the building, although, by 1900, the post office had moved one block north to Sixth and Washington Streets. Today First Financial Bank occupies the former Irwin Union Bank building, which was designed in 1954 by Eliel Saarinen as an innovative type of bank building with glass walls and an open interior floor plan.

The Columbus Kiwanis Club poses in front of the interurban streetcar near Washington and Third Streets in this early view (above). The interurban station was located in the building right behind the train across from the courthouse. In the 1970s, this block was cleared for the construction of the Commons (a retail and community performance space). The image below shows the Commons (with part of the courthouse visible in the background) prior to 2007, when it was torn down as part of a complete overhaul of the space.

The view looking west on Third Street has changed dramatically between this stereoscope view from 1874 (above) and today (below). At the left in the early view is the newly constructed courthouse before the tower clock was installed in 1875. At the end of the street was the Schwartzkopf Home (see page 81) that stood on what was called Tipton Hill. In 2010, the site of the Commons (currently being rebuilt) is on the right, but the end of Third Street now curves around to the Third Street Bridge. (Then image used by permission of the New York City Public Library.)

Another old view of Third Street looking west is taken from a slightly different vantage point than the historical picture, taken around 1910. This view shows the Crump Theater, which was opened in 1889 by Columbus businessman John Crump. The theater was used for live performances, silent films, and eventually talking pictures. Today the theater houses concerts and special events. Crump also created the city's first streetcar system in 1890, and one of his electric trolley cars is visible in the older view.

The Bissell Hotel stood on the corner of Third and Franklin Streets until John Crump remodeled it and renamed it the Belvedere Hotel in the 1890s, after opening his theater across the street. The structure was destroyed by fire in 1967 but was rebuilt. It was eventually sold to the county and now houses county offices. In the pre-1900 view from a stereoscope card, the McEwen-Samuels-Marr House is just visible on Third Street. The home was built in the mid- to late 1800s. It has been renovated and now serves as the home of the Bartholomew County Historical Society.

This page shows the view north on Washington Street from Third Street. Both views show the original Irwin's Bank building on the right on the corner. The early view shows an interurban car stopped at the intersection, as the interurban station was the first building on the left on Washington Street where a sign for "hotel" can be seen. All the buildings on the block on the left were demolished in the 1970s to make room for the Commons.

These views show the west side of Washington Street between Fourth and Fifth Streets during parades in 1902 (above) and 2009 (below). Hilger and Sons was started in 1884 by Andrew Hilger, a tailor who moved to Columbus in 1874. Later his son, Joseph Hilger, owned a dry-goods store, which moved to this building on Washington street in the 1880s. Joseph Hilger's store, which became known as the White House, started in the corner of the building by the alley but eventually expanded to include an entire third of the block and was in business until 1969. A variety of businesses occupy this block today.

CHAPTER 3

BUSINESSES

The American Starch Works Company had a large factory located on the northwest corner of Washington and Sixteenth Streets. The company was founded sometime before 1890, when the city directory lists its location as "n end of Washington." Some of the company's products included corn syrup, caramel coloring, and food starch. Today the area west of Washington Street at Sixteenth Street is a residential area and green space.

Mooney's Tannery was started in 1837 and moved to the west end of Fifth Street in 1863. The business employed 75 people and was considered the largest tannery in the world in the late 1800s. Mooney's closed in 1962, and the building was demolished in 1963. The early view (below) shows a wagon with a load of hides in front of the railroad tracks with part of the Cerealine Mill on the right. Today the railroad tracks run along Brown Street, which separates Mill Race Park and the Cummins, Inc., parking lot.

In the 1880s, the Cerealine Mill on Jackson Street operated next to the Pennsylvania Railroad. The company produced a dry breakfast cereal that was never a commercial success, and the building was abandoned in 1892. The railroad building was razed in the 1950s. The back portion of the Cerealine building was demolished in 1960, but the taller section remained. When Cummins, Inc., built its new corporate offices here in 1983, architects Roche Dinkeloo and Associates incorporated the Cerealine building into the design.

The Reeves family started two companies in the late 1800s, manufacturing agricultural implements and split wood pulleys, which were used to power factory machines before electric motors. Later Reeves produced variable-speed transmissions for use in early automobiles. The company later merged and was bought out but continued using this Seventh Street building until 2001. The building was then renovated and now houses law offices and storage space.

Cummins Engine Company was incorporated in 1919 by W. G. Irwin and Clessie Cummins, an inventor who worked as a chauffeur for the Irwin family. The company's early headquarters was located at the east end of Fifth Street in a house around which the first manufacturing plant was built (see page 3). This page shows the east end of Fifth Street in 1942 (below) and today (above). (Photograph used by permission of Lyle Cummins, son of Clessie Cummins.)

Zaharako's candy store opened in 1900 at 329 Washington Street. Mexican onyx soda fountains, used at the 1904 St. Louis World's Fair, were installed in 1905. The shop was also well-known for a full concert Welte German pipe organ, which was imported in 1908 and is still in use today. The Zaharako family continued to run the store for more than 100 years, and the store was affectionately known by locals as "the Greek's." The renovated Zaharako's reopened in 2009 and is now a soda fountain and a museum.

Joseph Gysie operated the Manhattan Clothing Company at 416 Washington Street in a building constructed before 1896 on part of Columbus founder John Tipton's original land. Charles F. Dell and his two brothers, Nicholas and William Dell, bought the store in 1916, and it became known as Dell Brothers. Today Charles F. Dell's grandson, Tom Dell, manages the store. Early on, as many as 15 employees worked in the busy store, which stayed open late on Saturdays so patrons who had just received their paychecks could shop.

The St. Denis Hotel was built around 1875 at Fifth and Washington Streets. In 1915, every room had electric lights, steam heat, and hot and cold water. The building once had a tower, which was removed sometime after Union Trust purchased it around 1923. The St. Denis Hotel continued to operate in part of the building for many years, and the clock on the corner of the building was a well-known downtown sight until the late 1950s. Over the years, this building has housed other banks, drugstores, tailoring shops, and a telephone company.

First National Bank was organized by the Crump family in 1865 as a local bank. The bank had two earlier homes but occupied this building (shown below) at Fourth and Washington Streets by 1875. Many prominent Columbus citizens served as president of the bank over the years, including William Lucas, F. T. Crump, F. J. Crump, Elizabeth Lucas (William's widow and the first female bank president in Indiana), and Frances Overstreet. First National Bank remained at this location into the 1980s. Today National City Bank occupies the building.

The Ulrich Block on the north side of Fourth Street between Washington and Franklin Streets was also known for many years as the White Star Building, as the White Star Meat Market occupied the corner location. The building can be seen in the bird's-eye view from the 1880s on page 24. Various businesses occupied parts of the block, including the piano company and a grocery store at this same location. Reportedly a brothel could be found upstairs in the building at one time.

Unger Monuments stood across Fourth Street from the Ulrich Building. Longtime Columbus residents remember the dust in the alley as stone monuments were cut behind the store. Unger Monuments was established prior to 1890, and business continued at this location until around 1962, when the company merged with another monument company. The early view was taken around 1930s, as Hinkle's Sandwich Shop (which later became Lucas Brothers) is visible to the left. Sometime after 1962, these buildings were demolished, and this is a parking lot today.

This building is unmistakable at 520 Washington Street both around 1910 (at right) and today (below). Columbus Cleaning and Dye Works is listed in the 1908 city directory on Fifth Street and run by Carl Schoessel. By 1913, Schoessel Cleaners is listed at the Fifth Street address, and Columbus Cleaning can no longer be found. Although the stairway is no longer present, the ornamentation on the building's facade has not changed.

Carl Schoessel eventually opened his own dry-cleaning business, and the 1913 city directory lists Schoessel Cleaners at 411 Fifth Street. (The street number is on the sign above the door.) By 1915, Schoessel Cleaners had moved to 508 Washington. The building's angle is unusual because it was located next to the diagonal alleyway where the railroad tracks had previously run from Fifth Street through to Railroad Square (see page 50). The original alley no longer exists, and the modern photograph shows the back of the bank building on the southeast corner of Fifth and Washington Streets.

The H. L. Rost Jewelry store was established in 1878 and occupied two different buildings on Washington Street before moving into this building on the southeast corner of Fifth and Washington Streets in 1906. The jewelry store was present on this corner until the early 1970s, after which various banks and other businesses occupied the corner. On the cover, the building is visible as it was up until September 2009, when Irwin Union Bank failed and was taken over by First Financial Bank.

Jack O'Bryan operated a jewelry store in Columbus from the 1920s until the 1950s, beginning on Fourth Street and eventually moving to 425 Washington Street. This picture (above) was taken in the Washington Street building, and O'Bryan can be seen standing on the left. The business sold jewelry, watches, and fountain pens. Today the building is home to an Italian restaurant, Tre Bicchieri, and the distinctive ornamental ceiling has been preserved.

These views show the northeast corner of Fifth and Washington Streets. Isaac M. and Isaac T. Brown established a weekly newspaper in 1872 and a daily paper in 1877. By 1890, the *Evening Republican* had moved to this building and cost $5 per year for six-day-a-week service. The building appears "cut off" at the corner, because the train tracks diagonally crossed Washington Street here to go to Railroad Square. Today the Columbus newspaper is called the *Republic,* and the Brown family still owns the paper's parent company.

On Fifth Street between Washington Street and the Irwin Block, the Knights of Pythius fraternal lodge building was constructed before 1910. It housed at least three different theaters over the years, including the Orpheum, the American, and then the Rio Theater in the 1940s and 1950s. The building was eventually torn down for the construction of Home Federal Bank (now Indiana Bank and Trust) and its parking lot on the corner of Washington and Fifth Streets.

The Independent Order of Odd Fellows Building at 605 Washington Street was constructed in 1893. The IOOF lettering is still visible on the building's facade. For many years, the building served as the Hoover Furniture Store, selling all sorts of home furnishings and appliances. A Hoover advertisement in 1916 stated, "We Can Furnish Your Home Complete For a Dollar or Two a Week." Over the years, many other businesses have occupied this building, and today a travel agency is located on the first floor.

Joseph Irwin established Irwin's Bank in 1871 within a dry-goods store he operated on Washington Street. Reportedly farmers asked Irwin to safeguard their money because his was the largest safe in town, and the bank became successful. In 1881, the bank moved to this building at Third and Washington Streets, and in 1928, Irwin's Bank merged with Union Trust (see page 42) and became Irwin Union Trust Company. Irwin Union was a fixture in Columbus until 2009.

The Reliance Manufacturing Company was an important supplier of military uniforms during both World Wars, and the company made more than one million uniforms in World War II alone. Reliance had factories all over and headquarters in Chicago. For many years, Columbus residents called this building "the shirt factory." The building has had many other uses, including as an antique mall, and currently it is subdivided into many smaller spaces occupied by a variety of businesses.

A. E. "Junie" Schumaker started what is now Coca-Cola Bottling in 1912 on Jackson Street. The company originally had only fruit-flavored soft drinks but, in 1914, expanded to ice cream. In 1916, the company obtained a license to bottle and distribute Coca-Cola in Bartholomew County and the surrounding area. This plant on Washington Street was built in 1942 and later expanded. In 1956, Schumaker sold the business to his son, Albert H. Schumaker. Both men can be seen standing in front of the plant in the early photograph.

This building on Sycamore Street was initially called J. Bruning Sycamore Grocery and Bakery and then later Joslin and Son Grocery and Market. The 1890 city directory advertised the store as a source for "groceries, provisions and queensware."

The building is located just across from the original St. Bartholomew Church between Seventh and Eighth Streets. Today the building and its distinctive facade remains, although it is not in use.

The Orinoco Furniture Company was started in 1890 and was sold in 1892 to a group of investors, including W. H. Lincoln. Lincoln and his brother-in-law George Lucas headed the company—which employed as many as 600 people—for many years in this building on Seventeenth Street. The company had a reputation for producing elegant, finely crafted dining room and bedroom furniture. In 1913, the Lincoln Chair Company was a spin-off from Orinoco Furniture, making chairs to go with Orinoco pieces. The years of the Great Depression were hard on the companies, and the businesses were closed by 1940.

The Lincoln Chair building on Thirteenth Street became the headquarters of Noblitt-Sparks in 1940. Q. G. Noblitt had started Noblitt-Sparks under a different name in 1919. In 1950, the company became Arvin Industries in this same building. Arvin produced various automotive parts (including tire pumps, heaters, mufflers, and exhaust systems) throughout its history and, for many years, also produced household goods (including fans, heaters, and radios). In 2000, Arvin merged with Meritor, and its presence in Columbus eventually declined. A devastating fire on Christmas Eve 2009 destroyed much of the building.

Becker's A & W Root Beer stand opened on Twenty-fifth Street in 1949. It was quickly a popular place for kids and teens. In the early photograph (below), boys crowd in after a Saturday morning football game. A tornado damaged the building in 1970, but a new building was constructed on the same spot. Today Becker's remains in the Becker family as a drive-in restaurant and is still popular with students from the nearby high school.

Central Garage (later Voelz Motors) was located at 314–316 Fourth Street in the early 1900s. This picture was taken around 1920. At some point the entire block was cleared for a parking lot in the late 20th century, but then a new parking garage was built here with retail businesses opening on the ground floor in 2009. Today Bistro 310 restaurant stands in this spot next to the alley.

CHAPTER 4

CHURCHES
AND SCHOOLS

The Central Conservatory of Music was located on the southeast corner of Ninth and Chestnut Streets in the late 1800s and run by William Bates. This picture was taken in 1876, and in 1882, the school advertised that its students "will be sure to learn nothing that they will have to unlearn." It is unclear when the building was demolished, but the 1890 city directory no longer lists the school. Today no trace remains of this impressive building.

The original Central School—also called Old Central—was built in 1859 and was located on Pearl Street between Sixth and Seventh Streets. The building housed elementary through high school students, and both the building and playground were segregated into separate sections for white and black students. The building was demolished in 1904 when a new Central High School was constructed on the same block, this time facing Seventh Street. Today the third Central School built in Columbus is visible across the lot where Old Central once stood.

CHURCHES AND SCHOOLS

Local architect Charles Sparrell, who also designed the old city hall, designed Washington School in 1886 on Pearl Street between Seventh and Eighth Streets. This was the first building in Columbus constructed especially to serve as a high school. When Old Central was replaced with a new Central High School in 1905, elementary students moved here. In the 1940s, the building was used for high school choir and band classes, and today the building has been converted to apartments.

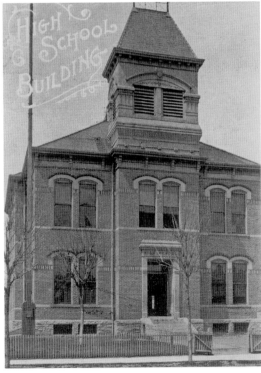

The "new" Central School opened in 1905 and served Columbus for more than 100 years, first as a high school and eventually as a middle school. The school originally had a dirt floor gymnasium in the basement and an auditorium on the third floor. A fire in 1979 caused significant damage, but the building was repaired and used until it was demolished in 2007 and a third Central built. Standing in front of where the old school stood offers a view across the new football field to the old and new St. Peter's Lutheran Church.

This page shows the construction of Maple Grove School—later called Garfield Elementary—in 1896 on Cottage Avenue. The building was designed by Charles Sparrell and served as an elementary school from 1896 until 1969. In 1988, the building was remodeled and expanded to become the headquarters of Arvin Industries, whose previous headquarters was a block away (see page 58). Today the restored building houses the school corporation offices.

First Presbyterian Church was organized in 1824, but its first building was located on Third Street. This building was constructed between 1871 and 1875 at Seventh and Franklin Streets. Although the church has undergone renovations and remodeling, this original structure remains essentially unchanged on the outside. The building can also be seen in the bird's-eye view picture from the 1890s on page 24.

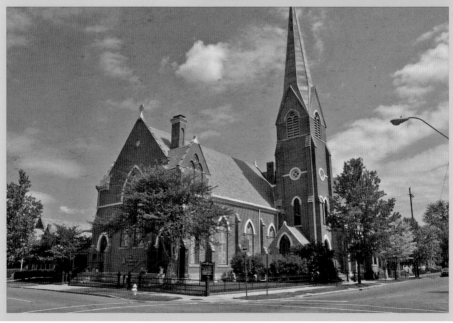

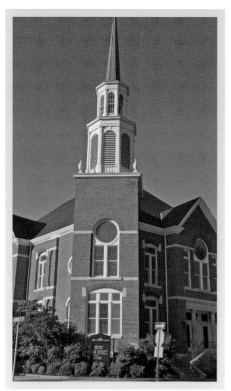

Originally called the Methodist Episcopal Church, First Methodist Church was another building designed by Charles Sparrell. This building was dedicated in 1887 and still stands at the corner of Eighth and Lafayette Streets, although it has undergone several major renovations, including in 1930, when the entrance was moved from under the steeple to the side of the building along Eighth Street. Although many original features of the building remain, the newer narrower steeple has changed the look of the church dramatically.

Originally called German Lutheran Church, St. Peter's Lutheran Church was built in 1870 at a cost of $9,000 at Fifth and Sycamore Streets and was one of five different German Lutheran congregations in the county at the time. The brick school behind the church was built in 1887. In 1988, architect Gunnar Birkerts designed a new St. Peter's adjacent to the original church.

CHURCHES AND SCHOOLS

St. Bartholomew Catholic Church was built around 1890 on Sycamore Street after an earlier Catholic church was located on Washington Street. By the 1920s, a Catholic school had opened next to the church. In the 1960s, a new church, called St. Columba, was built on the north side of Columbus, and the school moved there. This building was used until it was decommissioned and sold in 2002. Around the same time, the 1960s church was also demolished and rebuilt, and the new church on the north side of town then became known at St. Bartholomew.

Designed by Charles Sparrell, Central Christian Church was completed in 1886 on Seventh Street between Lafayette and Pearl Streets. The building was only used as a church for a few years, and by 1915, there were no regular church services. Over the years, it was also used as a recreation center by the Lutheran Church and even had a bowling alley. Today the building has been converted into apartments.

The English Lutheran Church was organized in 1893 at Eleventh and Chestnut Streets. An Orinoco streetcar, which ran between downtown and the Orinoco district, can be seen in the early view (see page 32). The picture at left was taken between 1893 and 1898 and was a popular subject of early postcards from Columbus. Today the building is still standing and is home to Calvary Community Church.

When the Tabernacle Christian Church needed a larger building in the late 1930s, church member J. Irwin Miller (later head of Cummins, Inc.) began to consider the idea of experimenting with modern architecture for the new structure. The new Tabernacle Church of Christ was designed by renowned architect Eliel Saarinen and opened in 1942 on the site of the former railroad square and Central Park. This was the first significant example of modern architecture in Columbus. In the early view below, the old Tabernacle is still visible in the background. A reflecting pool next to the church was eventually replaced with a courtyard and playground. Today the church is known as First Christian Church.

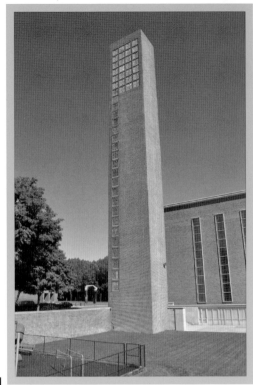

North Christian Church was designed by Eero Saarinen, son of Eliel Saarinen. Eero was well-known as the designer of Gateway Arch in St. Louis, and he finished his design for the church in 1961 but died before construction began. During construction the congregation met in the Caldwell home on Twenty-fifth Street (see page 92) until the church's completion in 1964. The church has a distinctive hexagonal shape and a 192-foot spire.

Asbury Methodist Church was built in 1955 and 1956 on Twenty-seventh Street at Forest Drive. The church was designed by one of its members, local architect Dean Taylor. Most of the 87 charter members came from First Methodist Church, but the first pastor and several members also canvassed the north side of Columbus looking for new members. The current sanctuary was built in 1966 and has many large windows and a 16-foot cross hanging from the ceiling.

CHAPTER

5

PARKS AND
OUTDOOR SCENES

In the early to mid-1900s, the area west of downtown between Mooney's Tannery and the river was known as Death Valley, where various shanties and shacks provided some shelter for many of Columbus's poorer citizens. Besides the social stigma of living in Death Valley, residents had to contend with frequent floods. In the 1960s, $150,000 was raised to buy and clear the area, and Mill Race Park was developed. This photograph was taken in 1900 and shows a boat on White River near Death Valley, with the courthouse in the background.

Garland Brook Cemetery was opened in 1886 on Tenth Street, well outside of what was then considered Columbus. The first burial was celebrated in the *Evening Republican* newspaper, and the vast open area beyond the gate in the early view stands in contrast to the crowded space of today. By 2008, Garland Brook had seen more than 27,000 burials since its opening, with projected space for 50 more years. Although this early gate is still standing, it is no longer an entrance to the property.

The park in the early view was known by various names—including Commercial Park, Central Park, and City Park—and was built on the former railroad square. In the background city hall is visible. The park had a large fountain and, at one time, a bandstand for Friday night concerts. In the 1940s, the park became the home for the new Tabernacle church, and the church's former home behind the library then served as a park for some years until the new library was built in the 1960s. Today the old city hall building can still be seen looking across the courtyard from First Christian Church.

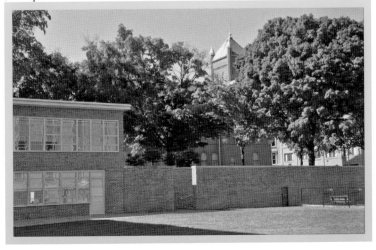

Donner Pool has been a popular place for the children of Columbus since the 1940s. The original 50-meter pool still looks much the same, although a slide and baby pool were added. The local swim club still uses the pool in summer also. Donner Pool sits within the large Donner Park, on Twenty-second Street between Sycamore and Lafayette Streets. Philanthropist Will Donner donated land for the park that bears his name in the 1920s.

The Lincoln Center Ice Rink opened in 1958 on Twenty-fifth Street. The building was designed by renowned architect Harry Weese, but the large rink was uncovered at the time, and the area around the rink was largely undeveloped. The rink was enclosed in 1976 and renamed the Hamilton Center (after the family who donated the land) in the 1990s. Today the building includes two rinks and houses ice-skating and hockey lessons and competitions.

In 1935, Q. G. Noblitt (cofounder of Arvin Industries) gave 75 wooded acres west of town to establish Columbus Youth Camp. Federal money from the Works Progress Administration (WPA) was used to pay some of the costs of building the 9-acre lake, buildings, and roads on the property. Lowell Engelking donated 40 more acres in 1958. Today the Youth Camp continues to be used for overnight and day camps for children and groups in Columbus.

CHAPTER 6

HOMES

Gen. John Tipton, a city founder, built his cabin on the city's highest point, called Tipton Hill (see page 30). This home was built sometime later but before 1885 and was known as the Schwartzkopf Home. Eventually it also served as the VFW headquarters before the home was demolished and the hill was leveled in 1950 for the construction of the Third Street Bridge.

The Lucas Home was located at Ninth and Washington Streets and was built between 1875 and 1879. Capt. William Lucas is seated in front, and his wife, Elizabeth, is standing in the doorway. Their daughter, Mary Crump Lucas, is standing in front of the window. Later the house was extensively remodeled when a porch was added, the tower removed, and the house greatly expanded. It was torn down in the 1950s, and an abandoned store stands in this spot today. Both Captain Lucas and his wife served as president of First National Bank (see page 43).

Originally the Crump family had a 95-acre farm that extended north from Eleventh Street and west of Washington Street, along with several houses on Jackson Street and Washington Street. This home—built in 1894 and 1895 at the corner of Eleventh and Washington Street—became known as the Overstreet Home, because First National Bank president Frances Overstreet lived here for much of the 20th century. Today it is home to Cindy's Picture Framing and Flower Market.

This large home was built on the northwest corner of Franklin and Seventh Streets in 1877 and was known as the Beatty-Donner Home. In the 1890s, it was described as the largest, most substantial, and most expensive home in Columbus. The Donner family (after whom Donner Park was later named) lived in the home for 50 years before it was eventually sold and razed to build a new telephone building.

The Irwin Home and Gardens, Columbus, Ind.

The original Irwin Home was built by Joseph Irwin on Fifth Street in 1864. A three-story entrance was added in the 1880s, and another remodel in the 1910s changed the home and added the sunken gardens, modeled after gardens in Italy. The last member of the original family to live here was Clementine Miller Tangeman, who died in 1996. The early view shows the original Tabernacle on the right, while the view today shows First Christian Church on the left.

This home at 825 Franklin Street was built between 1907 and 1913 in the prairie style by Edgar McSweeney, whose own home was just south of here. The house is full of finely crafted woodwork, including crown molding, built-in cabinetry, and wainscoting. The home was converted to apartments in 1929 and then returned to a single family residence by Nick and Cathy Rush, who bought the home in 1976.

The large home at 925 Franklin Street was built in the late 1800s by Joseph Gent, who was a partner in Gaff, Gent, and Thomas Cerealine Mill (see page 37). After the mills in Columbus closed, the home was bought and occupied for almost 50 years by H. L. Rost, a local jeweler (see page 48). The home was converted to apartments in the 1940s.

Also known as the Lambert-Noblitt Home, the Hill Crest Home was built from 1910 to 1914 on Washington Street. In 1928, the president of the H. C. Whitmer Company (see page 20), Fred Whitehouse, bought the home. In the 1940s, Q. G. Noblitt, one of the founders of Noblitt-Sparks (later Arvin Industries) bought the home. The exterior of the home has changed little over the years, although the home is no longer at the north edge of town, as Columbus has grown substantially.

"Hill Crest Home", Columbus, Ind.

This home at 2300 Washington Street was built by Mayme Crump Lucas, daughter of William Lucas (see page 82), and her husband in 1919–1920. The early view shows the house shortly after its construction. Later it was remodeled and a two-story portico was added, the roofline changed, and the carport removed. Members of the Reeves and Noblitt families lived here also before Dr. Marvin Davis bought the property in the 1950s and stayed here for many years. The home has been restored beautifully both inside and out.

The Perry-Reeves-Marr home at 2900 Washington Street was built in 1835 and was the only home north of the city limits on Washington Street for many years. It is one of the oldest buildings still standing in the county. Members of three early Columbus families occupied the home for more than 150 years until it was purchased in the 1980s by Mark and Marabeth Levett.

The Ruddick-Nugent House on Sixteenth Street was built in 1884 on 80 acres just outside the city limits. This early view was taken around 1890, with William Ruddick, second from the left and Elizabeth Ruddick (Nugent), far right, at age 16. She lived in the house for 86 years, remodeling it in 1924 to Greek Revival style. Dennis and Joyce Orwin restored the house from 1996 to 2005 as a bed-and-breakfast.

The stately home shown below was built in 1904 by a prominent local builder, George Caldwell, far outside city limits. Caldwell's most famous construction projects were several buildings at the 1904 St. Louis World's Fair and the West Baden Hotel in West Baden Springs, Indiana. The unpaved road later became Twenty-fifth Street, and the home stood at Twenty-fifth and Caldwell Streets until it was demolished in 1960. In the 1930s and 1940s, the home was a tearoom, a dance hall, a guesthouse, and even the first home of North Christian Church. Today a bank stands at this corner.

The Breeding Farm north of Columbus was built in 1871 after fire destroyed an earlier home on the site the previous year. Originally the home's kitchen was located in the basement. Henry Breeding owned the home—which was modernized in the early 20th century—from 1916 until his death in 1982, when the home was willed to the Bartholomew County Historical Society. Today the historical society still maintains the property, and the large barn houses parties, conferences, and weddings.

The John Storey Home at Fifth and Franklin Streets was built in the 1860s and is visible in the bird's-eye view on page 24. It housed a fraternal organization, a furniture store, and eventually the Boys Club, and the early view at right shows the building being repainted in the 1940s. Since the 1970s, the building has housed the Columbus Area Visitors Center. A major expansion occurred in the 1990s, and a large glass chandelier by Dale Chihuly hangs in the glass atrium between the old and new sections.

BIBLIOGRAPHY

Bartholomew County Steps through Time. Columbus, Indiana: The Republic, 2007.

Columbus: 125 Years. Columbus, Indiana: The Republic, 1997.

Columbus city directories, 1885–1965.

www.columbus.in.us

Cummins, Lyle. *The Diesel Odyssey of Clessie Cummins.* Wilsonville, Oregon: Carnot Press, 1998.

Fish, Henry. *Illustrated Columbus Indiana 1915.* Columbus: Commercial Club and Retail Merchants Association, 1915.

www.historiccolumbusindiana.org

www.irwinfinancial.com/corporate/history

Jones, Susanna, ed. *Bartholomew County Columbus, Indiana Sesquicentennial.* The Avery Press, Inc. 1971.

www.kiva.net/~garland

Marsh, William. *I Discover Columbus.* Oklahoma City: Semco Color Press, 1956.

Marshall, Robert J. and Jean Prather. *History of Bartholomew County Indiana Volume II 20th Century.* Columbus, Indiana: Pentzer Printing, 2003.

Marshall, Robert J., Ross G. Crump, and Mildred Murray, editors. *History of Bartholomew County Indiana Volume I 19th Century 1976 Annotated Edition.* Columbus, Indiana: Pentzer Printing, 1976.

Sanborn maps of Columbus Indiana, 1886-1827.

Souvenir Program: Grand Army of the Republic, Columbus, Ind. 1898. Reproduction. Evansville, Indiana: Unigraphic, 1980.

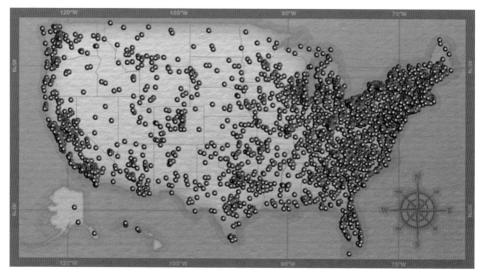